Forms for Report Writing

W9-COD-307

This volume provides one-and two-page report forms...
- to use with children beginning to do research
- to serve as simple reports on a wide variety of topics
- to use as a form of note-taking record in preparing to write longer formal reports
- to serve as notes for oral reports
- to use as part of a thematic unit of study
- to place in a science or social studies center

Each major subject area begins with a teacher resource page.

Many topics are also accompanied by clip art pages for your students to use as an addition to their report forms.

Table of Contents

Congratulations on your purchase of some of the finest teaching materials in the world.

Author: Jo Ellen Moore
Editor: Joy Evans
Designer: Jo Supancich

Entire contents copyright ©1994 by EVAN-MOOR CORP.
18 Lower Ragsdale Drive, Monterey, CA 93940-5746
Permission is hereby granted to the individual purchaser to reproduce student materials in this book for non-commercial individual or classroom use only. Permission is not granted for school-wide, or system-wide, reproduction of materials.

Evan-Moor
HELPING CHILDREN LEARN

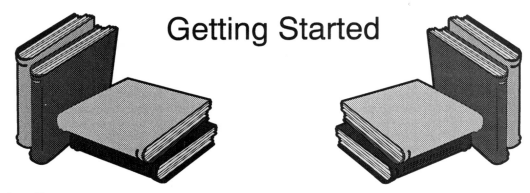

Getting Started

Model the Process:

Select a topic to use as a model for the process of locating information and writing concise answers.

If you have access to an overhead projector, make a copy of the report from on overlay film. You can then fill in the answers using an erasable felt marker such as Vis-a-Vis.

Reproduce a copy of the form for each child.

Read aloud from sources containing answers to the questions (one question at a time). Have children provide the answer from what you have read. Write the answer on the overlay. Have children copy the answer on their sheets.

You may need to model the process on more than one occasion for some groups of children.

Student Reports:

When you feel your students are ready, assign (or let them select) a topic. You may have children work independently, in pairs or in small groups.

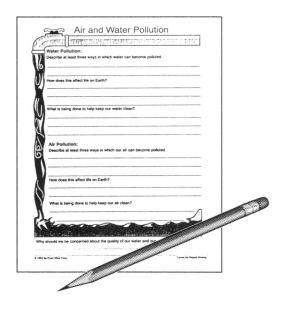

1. Reproduce the form/forms you need.
2. Provide research materials appropriate for the age and ability of your students. This may include setting up time for research in the library.
3. Discuss the questions ask on the form. Brainstorm possible ways to locate information.
4. Provide time for research and writing.

Formal Report Writing:

Finding answers and filling in the form is enough for younger students. Older, more-able students can use the forms as a starting point for writing a formal report. *Guided Report Writing* (EMC 221) provides an excellent resource for helping your students move from report forms such as the ones in this book, to writing complete, independent full-length reports.

Events

Teacher Preparation:

Check your school library to determine what resources are available for student use. Provide as many grade-appropriate materials as possible in the classroom. This should include books, magazines, audio-visual materials, newspaper articles, everything you can think of to provide adequate research possibilities.

Here are some suggestions of materials you might find in your school or public library:

School Events:
My New School by Hains; Kindersley/Houghton Mifflin, 1992.
Born in the Gravy by Cazet; Orchard, 1993.
Making the Grade (a series of books); Troll, 1992.

Current Events:
The American Scene: Ethnic America by Herda; Millbrook, 1991.
State Reports (a series of books); Chelsea House, 1992.
My Home Country (a series of books); Gareath Stevens, 1993.
Places in the News (a series of books); Crestwood House, 1992.

Historical Events:
Turning Points in American History (a series of books); Silver Burdett, 1991.
The Almanac of American History by Schlesinger; Putnam, 1983.
We Americans; National Geographic, 1975.
Spotlight on American History (a series of books); Milbrook Press, 1993.

With Students:

•Assign a specific topic or area of choices.
•Review the questions on the form/forms.
•Discuss available materials.

Brainstorm with your students to create a list of events they might choose. You may want to set some parameters since a topic such as "An Historical Event" is so broad. For example, instead of civil rights, a child might write about the March on Washington D.C.; instead of the discovery of America, a child might write about the voyage of Leif Erikson.

Choose an event which has occurred in school that is important to you and/or your classmates.

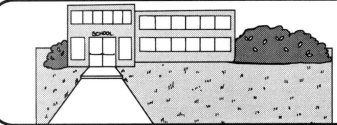

An Event at School

A Report by _____

When did this event take place? _____

Where did it happen? _____

Who was there? _____

Describe the event.
_____
_____
_____
_____
_____

What was the outcome of this event?
_____
_____
_____
_____
_____

What caused this event to occur?
_____
_____

Why was this event important to you and/or your classmates?
_____
_____

Illustrate the event here.

If you could change something about this event, what would it be?

_____
_____
_____
_____
_____
_____

Report on a Current Event

Look in the newspaper. Choose an event that interests you.

OUR TIMES

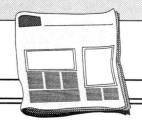

DATE: _____   Volume 1

Paste a headline here or create your own.

Event: _____
_____

Name the people involved in this event and describe their involvement.

_____
_____
_____
_____
_____

Briefly describe the main points of this event.

_____
_____
_____
_____
_____
_____
_____

List 4 reasons why this event is important.

_____
_____
_____

What are some probable outcomes of the event?

_____
_____
_____

An Event from History

_____
Name of Event

Basic Facts

When did this take place? _____

Where did it happen? _____

How long did it last? _____

Describe at least three important details of what happened during this event.

_____

_____

_____

How did this event affect the people?

_____

_____

_____

Why is this event important in history?

_____

_____

_____

List some of the most important people participating in this event.

_____   _____

_____   _____

_____   _____

Science

Teacher Preparation:

Check your school library to determine what resources are available for student use. Provide as many grade-appropriate materials as possible in the classroom. Here are some suggestions of materials you might find in your school or public library:

Human Body Systems:

Growing Up Healthy (Volumes 1-3) by Tothenberg; Danbury Press, 1976.

Freckly Feet and Itchy Knees by Rosen; Doubleday, 1990.

The Human Body (Prentice-Hall Dictionary); Prentice-Hall, 1992.

Outer Space and Constellations:

A Field Guide to the Stars and Planets by Menzel; Houghton, 1983.

Planetary Exploration Series; Facts on File, 1989.

Solar System: Opposing Viewpoints by Roop; Greenhaven, 1988.

Issac Asimov's Library of the Universe (a series); Dell, 1989.

Vertebrates and Invertebrates:

National Geographic Book of Mammals by Nat'l Geographic Society, 1981.

Invertebrates by Bander; Glouster, 1988.

Habitats:

Habitats: Where the Wild Things Live by Muir; Norton, 1992.

Physical Science:

Gravity: the Universal Force by Nardo; Lucent, 1991.

Environmental Awareness: Water Pollution by Snodgrass; Bancaroft/Sage, 1991.

Wonderful Water by Kalman; Crabtree, 1992.

The Audobon Society Field Guide to North American Rocks and Minerals by Chesterman; Knopf, 1978.

With Students:

•Assign a specific topic or area of choices.

•Review the questions on the form/forms.

•Discuss available materials.

Discuss the topic or topics on which your students will be reporting. Point out the type of resources they can use. Review how to take notes and how to compile the information from more than one source into sentences and/or paragraphs.

Note: Reproduce this and the following page for the report on a system of the body.

Report on a Body System

Systems you might choose:
____ skeletal
____ muscular
____ digestive
____ respiratory
____ circulatory
____ nervous
____ other

_____
name of system

What is the function of this system?

_____
_____
_____
_____
_____
_____
_____
_____
_____
_____
_____
_____

Draw or paste a picture of the system here.
Label the major parts.

List 3 ways you can help keep this system in good working order.

_____
_____
_____
_____
_____

Describe how the system works.

_____
_____
_____
_____
_____
_____
_____
_____
_____
_____
_____
_____
_____

How does this system interact with other systems in your body?

_____
_____
_____
_____
_____
_____
_____

Body Systems

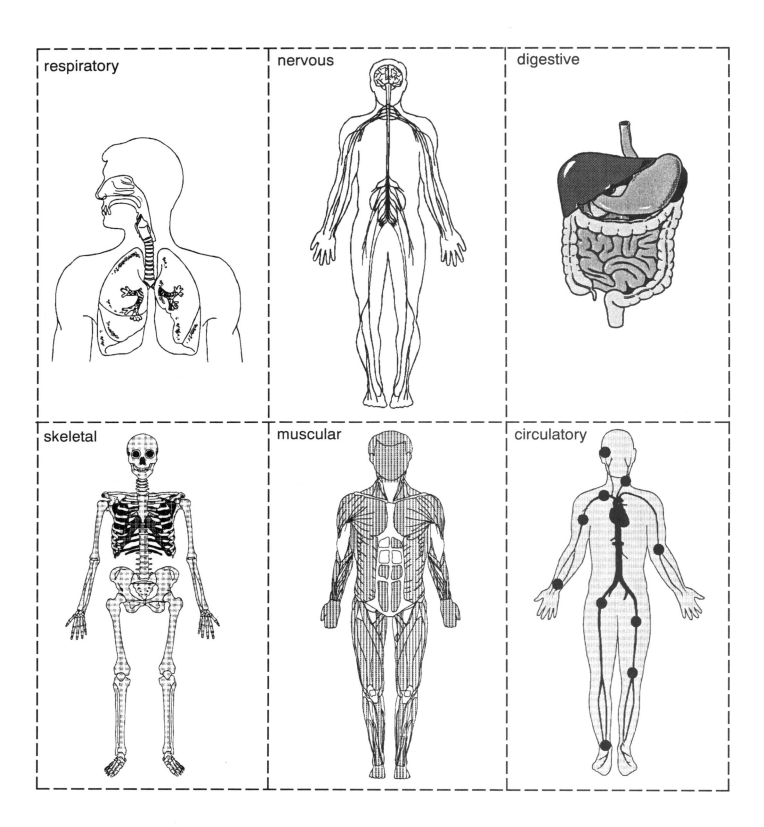

respiratory

nervous

digestive

skeletal

muscular

circulatory

Name of object/planet:

_____

Outer Space

Paste or draw a picture of the object/planet here.

Describe the physical structure of this object/planet.

_____

_____

_____

_____

_____

_____

_____

_____

_____

_____

_____

Where is this object/planet located? How far is it from the Sun?

_____

_____

_____

_____

_____

_____

_____

_____

_____

_____

List at least five important facts about this object/planet.

_____

_____

_____

_____

_____

_____

_____

How is this space object different from the Earth?
How is this space object like the Earth?

_____

_____

_____

_____

_____

_____

_____

_____

 Forms for Report Writing

Note: The planets are not to scale.

The Planets

Jupiter

Uranus

Earth

Mars

Neptune

Mercury

Venus

Pluto

Saturn

Forms for Report Writing

Clip Art

Objects in the Solar System

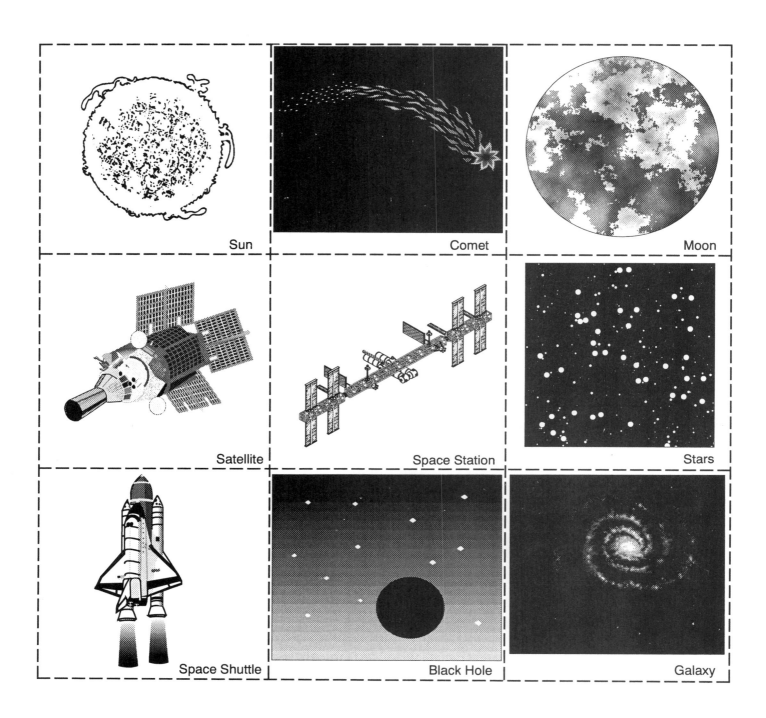

Sun

Comet

Moon

Satellite

Space Station

Stars

Space Shuttle

Black Hole

Galaxy

Forms for Report Writing

Constellations

Name of the constellation: _____

Describe this constellation.

_____

_____

_____

_____

_____

Paste or draw a picture of the constellation here.

Basic information:

Is it located in the northern or southern hemisphere? _____

How many stars are a part of the constellation? _____

Do any of the individual stars have names? If yes, list them. _____

_____ _____ _____

How far is the constellation from Earth? _____

What time of year can it be seen from where you live? _____

Explain how the constellation got its common name.

_____

_____

_____

_____

_____

_____

Constellations

Queen on a Throne
(Cassiopeia)

The Dragon
(Draco)

The Hunter
(Orion)

Big Dipper
(Ursa Major)

The Winged Horse
(Pegasus)

The Swan
(Cygnus)

The Fish
(Pisces)

The Lion
(Leo)

The Great Bear
(Ursa Major)

Note: Have books and other resource materials available for your students to use while completing this assignment.

Vertebrates Report

This animal is a...
___ reptile
___ mammal
___ bird
___ amphibian
___ fish

_____
name of animal

Describe the animal (physical characteristics).

_____
_____
_____
_____
_____

Draw or paste a picture of the animal here.

Describe where the animal lives (habitat).

_____
_____
_____
_____
_____

Draw a picture of its habitat.

Describe how the animal protects itself.

_____
_____
_____

Forms for Report Writing

Tell what you know about the animal's life cycle.
Illustrate the life cycle.

_____

_____

_____

_____

_____

_____

_____

_____

_____

Tell three more interesting facts about this animal.

The animal's favorite foods:

_____

_____

_____

_____

_____

_____

_____

_____

_____

_____

_____

_____

_____

Draw a picture showing one of its behaviors.

Mammals

Clip Art

Birds

cardinal

chicken

duck

eagle

hummingbird

parakeet

parrot

ostrich

swan

vulture

penguin

owl

Amphibians

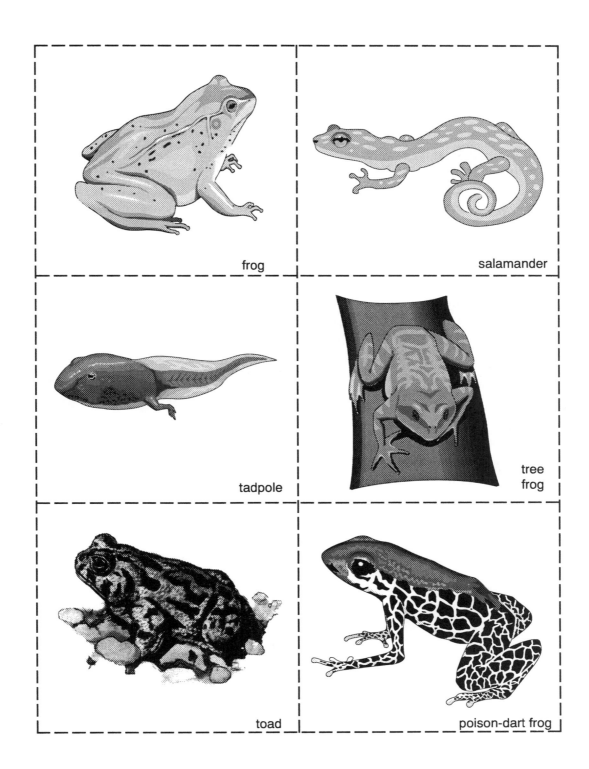

frog

salamander

tadpole

tree frog

toad

poison-dart frog

 Forms for Report Writing

Reptiles

horned toad

tortoise

alligator

chameleon

lizard

rattlesnake

Fish

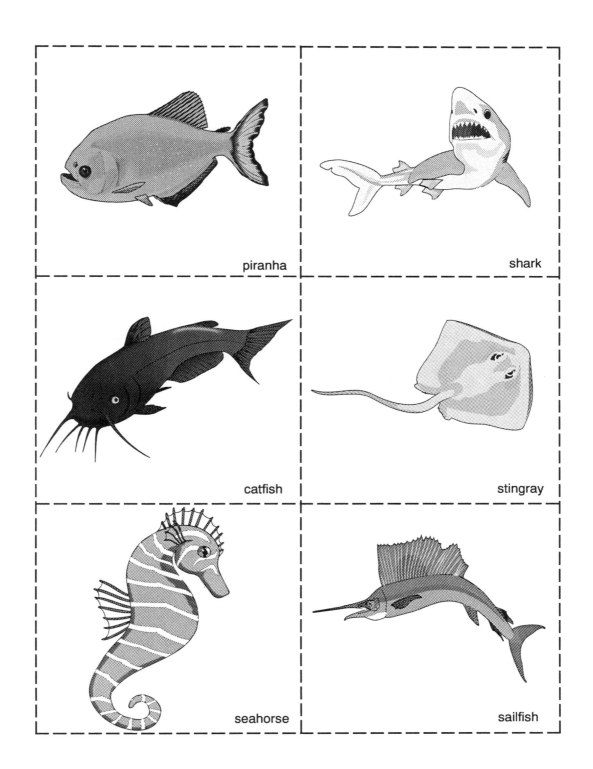

piranha

shark

catfish

stingray

seahorse

sailfish

 Forms for Report Writing

Note: Have books and other resource materials available for your students to use while completing this assignment.

A Report on

Invertebrates _____
name of animal

What is an invertebrate?

_____

_____

Describe how this invertebrate protects itself.

_____

_____

_____

Paste or draw a picture of the animal here.

Describe this invertebrate (physical characteristics).

_____

_____

_____

_____

_____

_____

List its favorite foods.

_____

_____

_____

_____

Describe where this invertebrate lives (habitat).

_____

_____

_____

_____

_____

Draw a picture of its habitat.

Tell what you know about this invertebrate's life cycle. Draw a picture of its life cycle.

_____

_____

_____

_____

Tell three more interesting facts about this invertebrate (behaviors).

1. _____

_____

2. _____

_____

3. _____

_____

Draw one of these behaviors.

Invertebrates

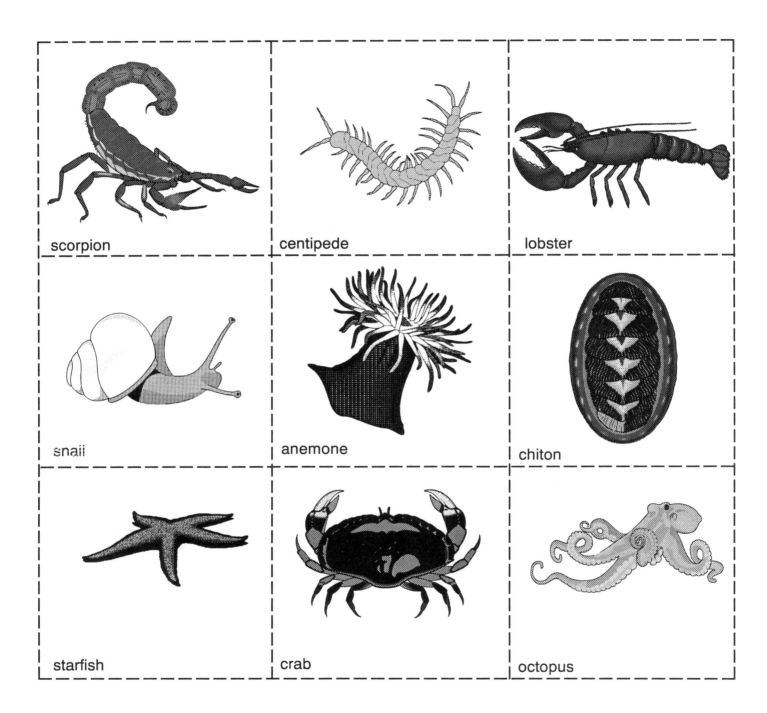

scorpion

centipede

lobster

snail

anemone

chiton

starfish

crab

octopus

Insects

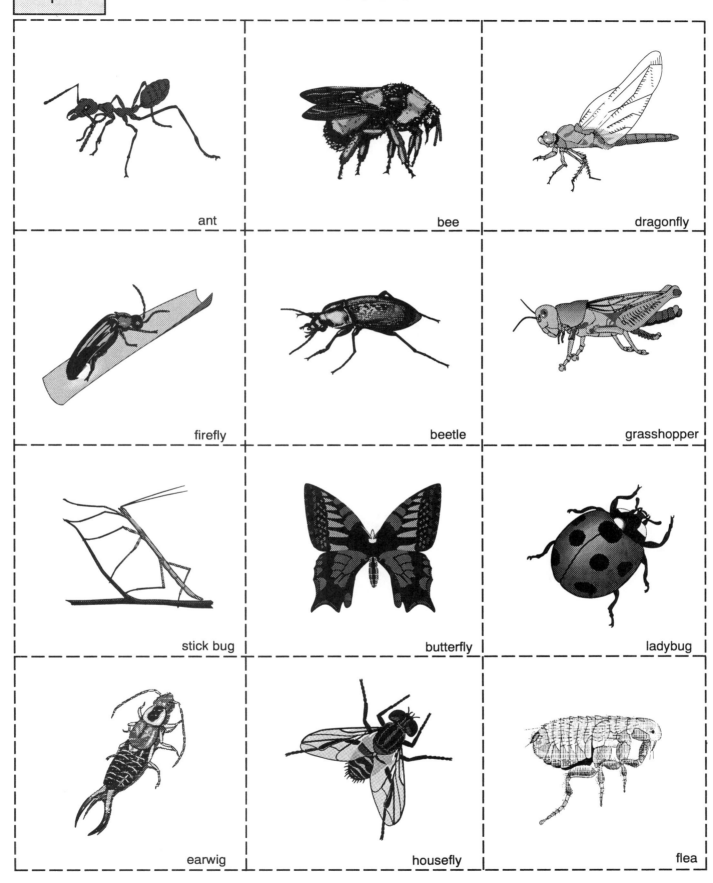

ant

bee

dragonfly

firefly

beetle

grasshopper

stick bug

butterfly

ladybug

earwig

housefly

flea

A Report by _____

Habitats you might choose:
___ desert
___ tropical rain forest
___ grassland
___ tundra
___ swamp
___ mountains
___ other

_____
name of habitat

A Habitat

Characteristics of this Habitat

1. Usual climate

_____
_____
_____

2. Land and water forms

_____
_____
_____

3. Major types of plant life

_____
_____
_____

4. Animals commonly found here

_____
_____
_____

Draw a picture of this type of habitat here.

Name at least three areas where this type of habitat is found.

_____

_____

_____

_____

Do any groups of people live in this habitat?
How have they affected the habitat?

A Report on Gravity

What is gravity?

_____

_____

_____

How do we know gravity exists?

_____

_____

_____

Describe the effect gravity has on the relationship between the Earth and its moon.

_____

_____

What did Galileo discover about gravity?

_____

_____

What did Issac Newton discover about gravity?

_____

_____

_____

_____

Draw a picture showing the effect of gravity.

Draw the same picture showing what would happen without gravity.

Describe what would happen if gravity ceased to exist.

_____

_____

_____

_____

States of Water

A Report by _____

What is the chemical formula for water? _____

What does this formula mean?_____

What effect does salt have on the boiling and freezing points of water? _____

What causes water to change from one form to another? _____

Name the three states in which water can be found. Write at least three facts about each form.	Illustrate water in each of its forms.
1. _____ _____ _____ _____	
2. _____ _____ _____	
3. _____ _____ _____	

Rocks

Select one type of rock:

___ sedimentary

___ igneous

___ metamorphic

Give three examples of this type of rock.

Describe how this rock is formed.

_____

_____

_____

_____

_____

_____

_____

_____

_____

_____

How can you tell one type of rock from another by just looking at it?

_____

_____

List at least five ways in which mankind uses rocks.

1._____

2._____

3._____

4._____

5._____

Sketch a sample of this type of rock.

What effect does moving wind and water have on rock formations?

_____

_____

Ecology

Teacher Preparation:

Check your school library to determine what resources are available for student use. Provide as many grade-appropriate materials as possible in the classroom. This should include books, magazines, audio-visual materials, newspaper articles, everything you can think of to provide adequate research possibilities.

Here are some suggestions of materials you might find in your school or public library:

Garbage:
Tons of Trash: Why you should recycle and what happens when you do by Heilman; Avon, 1992.
Environmental Awareness (a series) by Snodgrass; Bancroft/Sage, 1991.
Throw Away Generation by Wheeler; Abdo/Rockbottom, 1991.

Endangered Animals:
Animals in Danger by Amos; Raintree/Steck Vaughn, 1993.
Protecting Endangered Species by Brooks; EDC, 1990.
Endangered Habitats by Tesar; Facts on File, 1991.
Endangered Animal (a series) by Taylor; Crabtree, 1993.

Air and Water Pollution:
Polluting the Oceans by Bright; Glouster, 1991.
Acid Rain Hazard by Woodburn; Gareath Stevens, 1992.
Caring for Our Earth (a series) by Greene; Enslow, 1991.
Water Pollution by Stille; Childrens Press, 1990.

With Students:

• Assign a specific topic or area of choices.
• Review the questions on the form/forms.
• Discuss available materials.

Discuss the topic or topics on which your students will be reporting. Point out the type of resources they can use. Review how to take notes and how to compile the information from more than one source into sentences and/or paragraphs.

A Report by _____

Garbage

Describe what might be found in a can of garbage.

_____
_____
_____
_____
_____
_____
_____
_____
_____

Where does your garbage go once it has been picked up by the garbage collector? What happens when it reaches that destination?

_____
_____
_____
_____
_____
_____
_____

Does your community have a recycling program? If yes, describe it.

_____
_____

Does your community have a program for disposing of toxic waste items such as leftover paint and fertilizer containers? If yes, describe how it works.

_____
_____

Why should we be concerned about the amount and types of garbage created in our community? Describe what would happen if there was no place to dispose of the garbage in your community.

_____
_____
_____
_____

Endangered Animals

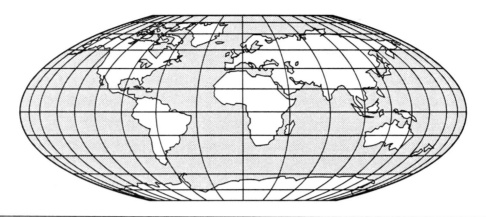

Name of the animal: _____

This animal lives on the continent/continents of _____
Color the continent green.

Current population of this animal: _____

Describe the animal.
(physical appearance) _____

_____

_____

_____

Describe the animal's habitat.

_____

_____

_____

_____

_____

_____

_____

Draw or paste a picture of the animal here.

List some interesting behaviors this animal shows.

_____

_____

_____

_____

_____

_____

_____

_____

_____

_____

Why is this animal endangered?
What is being done to save this animal?

_____

_____

_____

_____

_____

_____

_____

_____

_____

Why do you think it is/is not important that this endangered animal be saved?

_____

_____

_____

_____

_____

_____

_____

_____

_____

Endangered Animals

Mountain
Gorilla

African
Elephant

Bald Eagle

Black
Rhinoceros

Pygmy Hippopotamus

Sea Otter

California Condor

Giant Panda

Sea Turtle

Air and Water Pollution

Water Pollution:

Describe at least three ways in which water can become polluted.

_____

_____

How does this affect life on Earth?

_____

_____

What is being done to help keep our water clean?

_____

_____

_____

Air Pollution:

Describe at least three ways in which our air can become polluted.

_____

_____

How does this affect life on Earth?

_____

_____

What is being done to help keep our air clean?

_____

Why should we be concerned about the quality of our water and our air supply?

_____

Places

Teacher Preparation:

Check your school library to determine what resources are available for student use. Provide as many grade-appropriate materials as possible in the classroom. This should include books, magazines, audio-visual materials, newspaper articles, everything you can think of to provide adequate research possibilities. Here are some suggestions of materials you might find in your school or public library:

Geography from A to Z by Knowlton; Harper, 1988.
Continents by Fradin; Childrens Press, 1986.
Great Atlas of Discovery by Grant; Knopf/Random House, 1992.
Webster's New Geographical Dictionary; Merriam-Webster, 1984.
The World's Children (a series) by Harkonen; Carolrhoda, 1990.
Imagine Living Here (a series) by Cobb; Walker, 1989.
The Story of America: A National Geographic Picture Atlas; National Geographic, 1984.
Lake by Bender; Watts, 1989.
Lakes and Ponds by Santrey; Troll, 1985.
World's Oceans by Sandak; Watts, 1987.
Oceans by Simon; Morrow, 1990.
The Sea (a series); Bookwright, 1991.
Oceans by Whitefield; Viking, 1991.
National Parks (a New True Book) by Petersen; Childrens Press, 1992.
The New America's Wonderlands: Our National Park; National Geographic, 1975.
Man-Made Wonders of the World by Turner; Dillon, 1986.
Natural Wonders of the World by Naylor; Dillon, 1986.
Mountains by Vrbova; Troll, 1990.
Mountains and Volcanoes; Kingfisher, 1993.

With Students:

• Assign a specific topic or area of choices.
• Review the questions on the form/forms.
• Discuss available materials.

Discuss the topic or topics on which your students will be reporting. Point out the type of resources they can use. Review how to take notes and how to compile the information from more than one source into sentences and/or paragraphs.

A Report on a Continent

_____
name of the continent

Describe the major geographic features of this continent.
(features such as mountains, rivers, deserts, forests)

_____
_____
_____
_____

List some of the unusual animals found on this continent.

_____
_____
_____
_____
_____

Paste or draw a map of the continent here.

List any unusual plants found on this continent.

_____
_____
_____
_____
_____

Forms for Report Writing

How many countries form this continent?

_____

_____

List:

1. What major languages are spoken?

_____

_____

_____

_____

_____

2. What are the major religions of the people?

_____

_____

_____

_____

3. What are the major types of government?

_____

_____

_____

_____

_____

Describe the five most interesting facts you have learned about this continent.

1. _____

_____

2. _____

_____

3. _____

_____

4. _____

_____

5. _____

_____

6. _____

_____

Would you be interested in visiting this continent? Why?

_____

_____

_____

_____

Continents

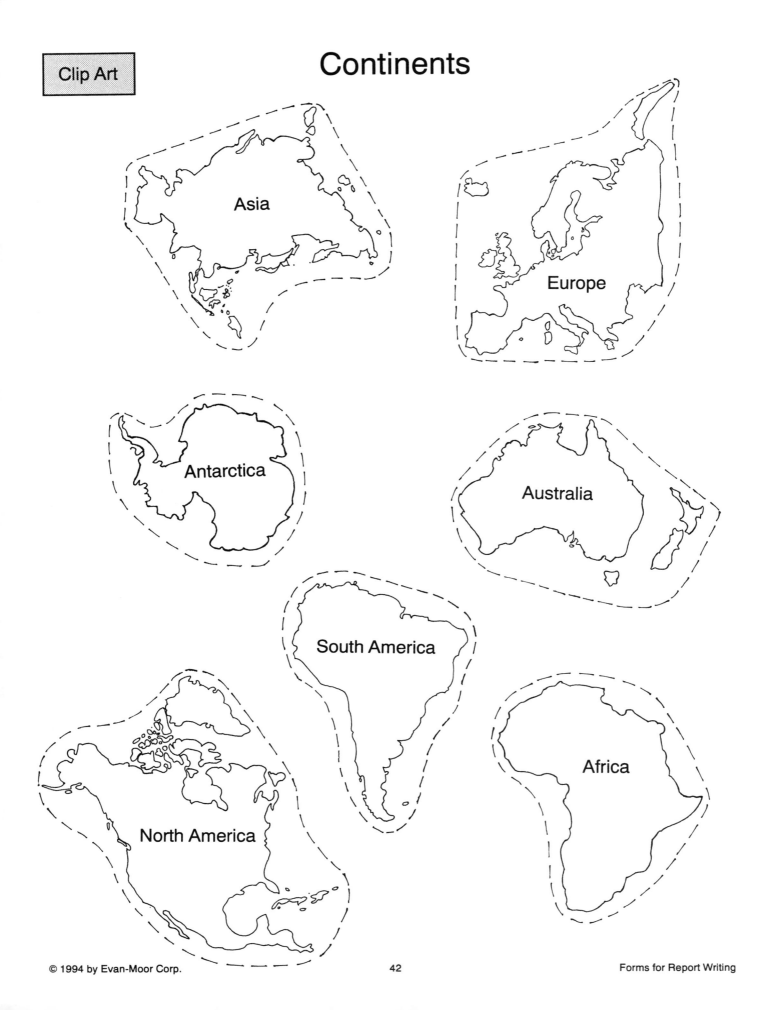

Asia

Europe

Antarctica

Australia

South America

North America

Africa

A Report on a Country

Basic Information

Country _____

Capital city _____

Population _____

Types of currency _____

Major languages spoken _____

Major religions _____

List the main products of this country.

_____ _____

_____ _____

_____ _____

Paste or draw a map of the country here.

Describe the type of government. Who is the current Head of State?

_____

_____

_____

_____

Name typical foods enjoyed by the people of this country.

_____

_____

_____

Describe the most unusual physical features of the country.
(such as mountains, lakes, forests, rivers)

_____

_____

_____

_____

List three or more unusual plants and animals found in this country.

_____

_____

_____

_____

_____

_____

_____

Describe a national holiday celebrated in this country.

_____

_____

_____

_____

_____

_____

_____

Describe three or more important facts you learned about this country and its people.

_____

_____

_____

_____

_____

_____

_____

Draw someone in the national dress.

State or Province Report

Basic Information

Name of State or Province _____

Capital city _____

Population _____

Major languages spoken _____

State/Province motto _____

Year state/province became part of the country _____

Paste or draw a map of the state/province here.
Draw and label two or more important physical features. (mountains, rivers, deserts, etc.)

List five of the main products of this state/province.

_____

_____

_____

_____

_____

List three or more important facts you learned about this state/province and its people.

_____

_____

_____

_____

_____

_____

Describe an important event from the history of this state/province.

_____

_____

_____

_____

_____

Draw the state/province flag here.

Draw the state/province bird here.

name
of
bird

Note: You may assign a lake in your area or to allow your students to select an interesting lake from anywhere in the world.

A Report on Lake _____

Where is this lake located? _____
_____

How deep is the lake? _____

How many miles/kilometers around is the lake? _____

Describe the three most important facts which make this lake interesting.

_____
_____
_____

What types of water plants and animals are found in this lake?

_____
_____
_____

Describe any industries that rely on this lake.

_____
_____

How many ways do people use the lake?

_____
_____

Describe any problems facing the lake.
Is anything being done to fix the problems?

_____
_____
_____
_____
_____

Draw a picture of the lake here.

Note: Reproduce the world map on the following page for children to use with this report.

A Report on an Ocean or Sea

_____
name of this body of water

What countries and islands are touched by this body of water?

_____
_____
_____
_____
_____

How do these countries and islands rely on this ocean or sea?

_____
_____
_____

What types of marine life are special to this ocean or sea?

_____
_____
_____
_____
_____

List three unique features of this ocean or sea.

1. _____

2. _____

3. _____

Map of the World

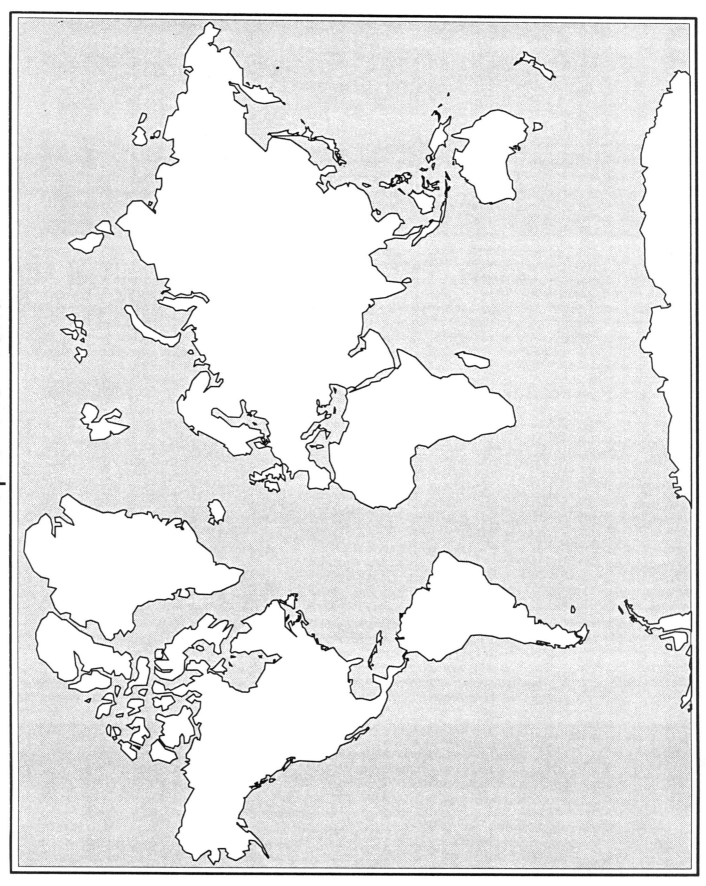

Forms for Report Writing

A Report on a National Park

name of park:

Location ——————————————————————

When established ——————————————————

Land or sea park ——————————————————

Why was this area named a national park?

_____

_____

Describe the environment.

_____

_____

Give at least five reasons this park is special.

_____

_____

_____

_____

_____

Describe some activities people can do at this park.

_____

_____

_____

_____

_____

_____

_____

Draw a picture that illustrates the special plant and animal life found in this park.

Have you ever been to this national park? If so, what did you like best about it?

_____

A Report on a National Monument

Name of monument:

_____

Monuments you might choose:

___ Washington Monument
___ Lincoln Memorial
___ Eiffel Tower
___ Statue of Liberty
___ Easter Island
___ The Sphinx
___ Taj Majal
___ Other

Draw or paste a picture the monument here.

Have you ever visited this monument?

___yes   ___ no

Where is it located? _____

When was it erected? _____

Who designed it? _____

Describe the monument.

_____

_____

_____

_____

_____

_____

_____

Describe the person, place or event for which this monument was erected.
What qualities about this person, place or event are being honored?

_____

_____

_____

_____

_____

National Monuments

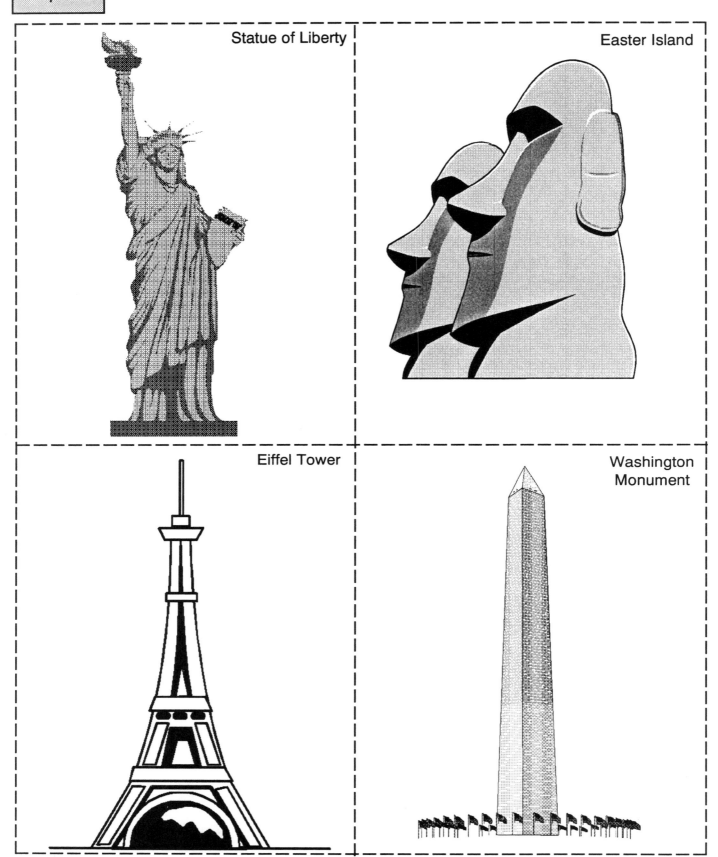

Statue of Liberty

Easter Island

Eiffel Tower

Washington
Monument

Forms for Report Writing

A Report on a Mountain Range

Mountain ranges you might choose:

___ Rocky Mountains
___ Andes Mountains
___ Himalayan Mountains
___ The Alps
___ Ural Mountains
___ Other

_____
name of this mountain range

On what continent are these mountains found?

_____

What is the highest peak in this range?

_____

What country/countries are touched by this mountain range?

_____

_____

_____

List any major cities located in these mountains.

_____

_____

_____

Describe the major physical features.

_____

_____

_____

Describe the vegetation found here.

_____

_____

_____

List some of the animals found here:

_____

_____

_____

What activities do people perform in these mountains?

_____

_____

Why is this mountain range important to people?

_____

_____

_____

People

Teacher Preparation:

Check your school library to determine what resources are available for student use. Provide as many grade-appropriate materials as possible in the classroom. This should include books, magazines, audio-visual materials, newspaper articles, everything you can think of to provide adequate research possibilities. Here are some suggestions of materials you might find in your school or public library:

Occupations:

Career Discovery Encyclopedia (six volumes); Ferguson, 1933.

All about Things People Do by Rice; Doubleday, 1990.

Historical Figures:

People and Places of the Past; National Geographic, 1983.

Webster's Biographical Dictionary; Merriam Webster, 1984.

Inventors:

Inventing (a series) by Bendick; Millbrook Press, 1992.

Outward Dreams: Black Inventors and their Inventions by Haskins; Bantam, 1991.

Inventors and Inventions by Jeffries; Smithmark, 1992.

Astronauts:

Astronauts by Burch; Garrett, 1992.

Space Exploration (a series); Facts on File, 1990.

Today's World in Space (a series) by Baker; Rourke, 1989.

Artists:

Getting to Know the World's Greatest Artists (a series) by Venezla; Childrens Press, 1990.

Weekend With... (a series;) Rizzoli, 1992.

The Arts (a series; Rouke, 1992.

President/Prime Minister:

President: America's Leader by Johnson; Raintree, 1993.

Encyclopedia of Presidents; Childrens Press, 1979.

Madam Prime Minister: A Biography of Margaret Thatcher by Hughes; Dillon, 1989.

Sports Figures:

For the Record: Women in Sports by Markel; World Almanac, 1985.

Achievers (sports biographies series); Lerner, 1992.

Olympic Gold (a series); Blackbirch, 1992.

With Students:

• Assign a specific topic or area of choices.

• Review the questions on the form/forms.

• Discuss available materials.

Discuss the topic or topics on which your students will be reporting. Point out the type of resources they can use. Review how to take notes and how to compile the information from more than one source into sentences and/or paragraphs.

Note: Reproduce this and the following page for a report on an occupation.

A Report on an Occupation

Name of occupation:

_____

What activities does this person perform?

_____

_____

_____

_____

_____

_____

_____

What training does this occupation require?

_____

_____

_____

_____

_____

_____

_____

_____

_____

What types of equipment are used in this occupation?

_____

_____

_____

_____

_____

_____

_____

In what type of environment does she/he work?

_____

_____

_____

_____

_____

_____

_____

_____

Interview someone with this job. What does she/he enjoy most about the occupation?

_____

_____

_____

_____

_____

_____

_____

_____

_____

What do you like about this occupation?

_____

_____

_____

_____

What do you dislike?

_____

_____

_____

Do you think you would like to do this when you grow up?

_____

_____

_____

Draw a picture of this person at work.

A Report about Myself

My complete name is:

_____

Basic Information about Me

I was born on _____ .
       date

I was born in _____ .
         city, state and country

I now live in _____ .
           city and state

There are _____ people in my family.

I am _____ years old.

I go to _____ School.

This is what I look like.

Four important events in my life are:

_____

_____

_____

_____

When I grow up, I want to be a _____ because I am interested in ...

_____

_____

I like to do these things in my free time:

_____

_____

_____

_____

Some of the things I like most about myself:

_____

_____

_____

A Report on a Person from History

People you might choose:

____ Paul Revere ____ Sojourner Truth
____ Chief Joseph ____ Winston Churchill
____ Archimedes ____ Mohandas Gandhi
____ Amelia Earhart ____ Malcolm X
____ Marco Polo ____ Montezuma
____ Muhammad ____ Other

Draw or paste a picture of the person here.

This person's name is:

_____

When did this person live? _____

Where did he/she live? _____

Why is this person remembered/famous?

_____

_____

_____

Describe three or more important events in his/her life.

_____

_____

_____

List some of his/her accomplishments.

_____

_____

_____

_____

How has this person affected our lives?

_____

_____

_____

_____

A Report about Someone in the News Today

Person's name _____

Country in which he/she lives: _____

Person's profession: _____

Age: _____

Is this person famous world-wide? _____

Where did you learn about this person?

___book   ___newspaper

___TV   _____

Draw or paste a picture of this person here.

Why was this person in the news?

_____

_____

_____

_____

_____

If you met this person, what would you ask them?

_____

_____

_____

Have you ever met this person?
Would you like to meet them? _____

A Report on an Inventor

Inventors you might choose:

___ Thomas Alva Edison
___ Galileo Galilei
___ Booker T. Washington
___ Garrett Morgan
___ Orville and Wilber Wright
___ Other

Name of the inventor:

_____

Draw or paste a picture of the inventor here with one of his/her inventions.

Where was she/he born? _____

In what year was she/he born? _____

Where did she/he live as an adult? _____

Where did she/he die? _____

In what year did she/he die? _____

What characteristics did this person have that helped her/him become a successful inventor?

_____

_____

Describe one or more of her/his inventions.

_____

_____

_____

How did this/these inventions help mankind?

_____

_____

_____

A REPORT ON AN ASTRONAUT

Astronaut's name: _____

Basic Facts

Where was he/she born? _____

In what year was he/she born? _____

Where did he/she live as an adult? _____

Describe the astronaut's childhood. _____
_____
_____
_____

How did he/she have to
train to become an astronaut? _____
_____
_____

What do you think was the
most important contribution
of this astronaut?
_____
_____
_____
_____

A Report on an Artist

Artists you might choose:

___ Leonardo da Vinci
___ Mary Cassatt
___ Edgar Allen Poe
___ Theodor Seuss Geisel
___ Duke Ellington
___ Michelangelo

___ Charlotte Bronte
___ Diego Rivera
___ Wolfgang Amadeus
___ Mozart
___ Fred Astaire
___ Other

Artist's name _____

Where was he/she born? _____

In what year was he/she born? _____

Where did he/she live as an adult?

_____

In what year did he/she die?

_____

What art forms did this artist use?
___ painting
___ sculpture
___ musical compositions
___ musical performance
___ written word

List some of this artist's important works:

1. _____

2. _____

3. _____

4. _____

Describe the artist's childhood.

_____

_____

_____

What do you think was the most important contribution of this artist?

_____

_____

A Report on a President or Prime Minister

Person's Name:

_____

This person was a: ___President   ___Prime Minister

What was his/her occupation before becoming President/ Prime Minister?

_____

_____

Basic Facts

Where was he/she born? _____

In what year was he/she born? _____

Where did this leader live as an adult? _____

When was he/she elected? _____

How long did he/she serve? _____

Describe the leader's childhood.

_____

_____

_____

_____

Describe at least three important events occurring during his/her years in office.

_____

_____

_____

_____

_____

_____

_____

What do you think was the most important contribution of this leader?

_____

_____

_____

_____

_____

_____

My Favorite Person in Sports

Basic Facts

Player's name:

_____

Sport he/she plays:

_____

Where was he/she born?

_____

When was he/she born?

_____

Tell something about his/her childhood.

_____

_____

_____

_____

_____

How did he/she become interested in this sport?

_____

_____

_____

Draw or paste a picture of the player here.

Why is he/she your favorite sports figure?

_____

_____

_____

_____

_____

Would you like to play this sport yourself? Why or why not?

_____

_____

_____

_____

What do you think was the most important contribution of this player?

_____

_____